7 Easy Steps t(
With 101 Music '
& 4 Mu(
A Companion for P1a..

Rosa Suen
Learn Piano With Rosa

7 Easy Steps to Read Music
With 101 Music Terms Dictionary
& 4 Music Charts
A Companion for Piano & Guitar Players

Author: Rosa Suen
Cover Design: Raymond Suen
Email: Rosa@LearnPianoWithRosa.com

Copyright 2013 By Learn Piano With Rosa Studio

All Rights Reserved. No part of this book (including the Videos material) may be reproduced, copied, stored, or transmitted in any form or by any means – graphic, electronic, or mechanical, including photocopying, recording, or in information storage and retrieval systems – without the prior written permission of Rosablanca Suen.

This ebook is licensed for your personal enjoyment only. This ebook may not be re-sold or given away to other people. If you would like to share this book with another person, please purchase an additional copy for each recipient.

About the Author

You can connect with me by visiting my Website:

1. Learn Piano With Rosa

2. My Piano Blog - Standards and Popular Songs

3. Dreamy Piano Courses and Fun Mini Lessons

4. My Online Piano Courses

5. Online Piano Courses at Udemy

Like me on my Facebook Page

I love to hear from you.

💡 You can write to me at: Rosa@LearnPianoWithRosa.com

Happy Piano Learning,

Rosa

Chapter I How To Read Music

Introduction:

Many people think that it is difficult to read music but it is NOT.

Music is actually the simplest written language for anyone to learn. Once you learn the basics, the reward is for a life time.

Learning how to read music is a significant step toward eventually being able to play the songs you want easily. This book will provide the music skills for you to read music at a basic level that you can play any song from a lead sheet. 101 Musical Terms are given to you so that you can also understand these terms easily.

This little book is to help beginners to read and interpret music notations easily in 7 easy steps.

Think of music as language, the notes can be compared to the letters of the alphabets. Just as we learn how to spell words, we also need to know how to interpret notes on scores.

Step 1   Start with Musical Staff

The MUSICAL STAFF is a set of 5 horizontal lines on which musical notes are written to indicate pitch and time. The staff is read from left to right. The higher the note is on the staff, the higher the pitch is being played. If a note appears above or below the 5 lines, LEDGER LINES are used to indicate the exact note.

The two main clefs are: TREBLE CLEF & Bass Clef

The treble clef is played with right hand. The bass clef is played with left hand.

My CCI method for piano players to play chords does not require you to read bass clef notations. All you need to know is to identify the notes on the keyboard and play chords with your LH. The keyboard diagrams in the lessons show you explicitly where to hit the keys on the piano so you do not need to read bass clefs at all. This is great news for all piano players.

Step 2   Read Treble Clef Notes

However, to play the melodic lines of a song, you need to learn to read the treble clef notes. Notes are written on the lines or spaces of the staff.

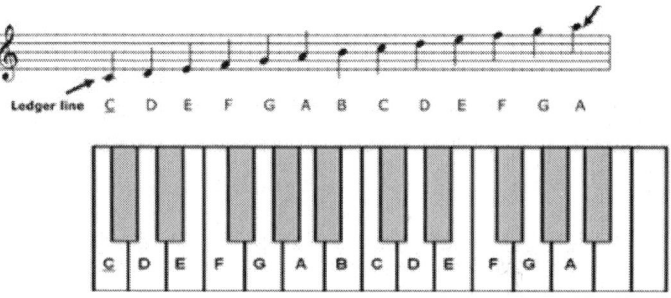

The middle C is underlined so that you can match the middle C to the middle C on the piano. When you see an F, you play the corresponding F on the piano. When you see a B, you play the corresponding B on the piano.

Step 3 Fast Trick Method to Identify Notes

Here is a little trick to help you identify notes faster:

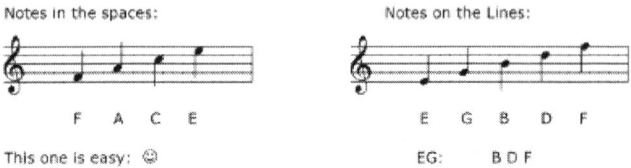

The spaces - gives you FACE.

The lines - give you : EG BDF

(Memorize EG as example. BDF is similar to "PDF", so we change the P to B for the sake of memory)

You only need to memorize the above to be able to read all the notes in the treble clef.

In the following pages, I give you exercises and tests. Do them and keep practising until you get 100% correct.

This is how you practice sight reading!

For Advanced Students - Reading beyond the ledger lines

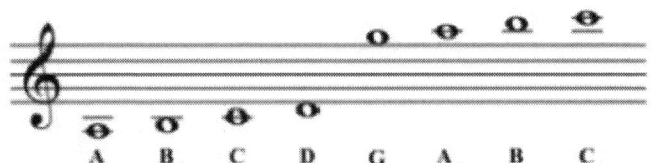

Memorize Below Ledger lines: **A B C D**
Memorize Above Ledger lines: **G A B C**

Practice Reading Treble Clef Notes

To play Chord Method or from fake books, all you need to learn is to read the Treble Clef Notes.

Do the following exercises and write your answer on a piece of paper. (Answer is provided for you on the next page)

Answer Key:
Here are the answers.
1. B A G
2. C A B
3. E G G
4. F E D
5. G A B
6. C A G E
7. F A D E
8. A G E
9. B E E
10. F A D
11. B E A D
12. E D G E
13. A C E
14. B E G
15. E B B
16. D E E D
17. F A C E
18. A D D

How many did you get correct?

If you manage to get only half right, go back to the previous page and do again. Keep doing the exercises until you get 90% correct. This is the way to practice reading notes.

Once you are able to get 90% correct, go to the next page and do the 'test'.

Test 1 - Write down the notes on a separate sheet of paper:

Hint Hint: I've made in such a way that each pitch spells a word.

This will give you some hint whether you got the answer correct or not.

Check the answer on the next page:

Answer to Test 1
They all spell a word.
1. F A C E
2. G A B
3. B A D E
4. F E E D
5. B E E
6. B E A D
7. B E E F
8. C A G E
9. B A G
10. C A B
11. D A B
12. C A F E
13. B A D
14. C A D
15. F A D
16. B E
17. C A G E
18. G A D
19. B E G
20. B E D
21. F E D
22. C E D E
23. A G E
24. A C E
25. F E E
26. A D
27. E D G E
28. F A D E

How many did you get correct?

If you manage to get only half right, go back to test 1 and do again until you get 90% correct. This is the way to practice reading notes.

Then you can move to the next test 2 - advanced.

Test 2 - More Advanced

Write down the notes on a separate sheet of paper:

Hint Hint: I've made in such a way that each pitch spells a word.

This will give you some hint whether you got the answer correct or not.

Check the answer on the next page:

Answer to Test 2

They all spell a word.
1. B A D G E
2. E G G E D
3. E B B E D
4. D E C A D E
5. D A E D
6. D E F A C E
7. C A G E D
8. E F F A C E
9. A D D E D
10. D A B B E D
11. A D A G E
12. F A C A D E
13. G A F F
14. C A B B A G E
15. D E A D
16. B A G G A G E
17. C A F E
18. E F F A C E D

How many did you get correct?

If you manage to get only half right, go back to test 1 and do again until you get 90% correct. This is the way to practice reading notes.

Step 4. Recognize White Keys & Black Keys

EACH BLACK NOTE is named in relation to its closest white notes. There are two names to each black key. For example, the black note between C and D is called either C# or Db. A sharp is when the note is raised a half-step. A flat is when the note is lowered half-step. We say C# and Db are enharmonic as they refer to the same tone but different name.

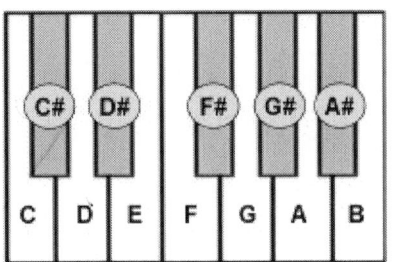

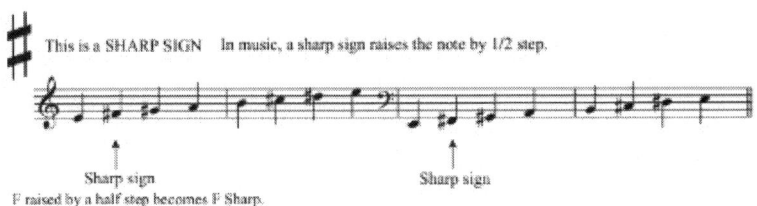

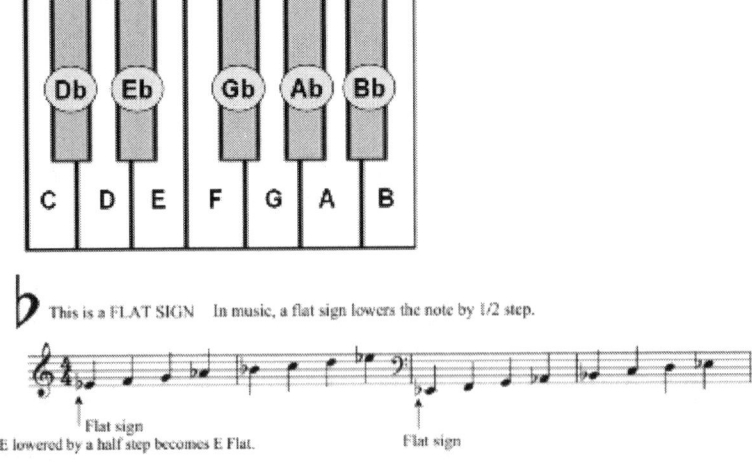

Once you understand the Sharps # and the Flats b, then you will understand how the scales are written.

Some scales are written in Sharps and some scales are written in Flats.

Scales with Sharps:

G Scale: G A B C D E F# G

D Scale: D E F# G A B C# D

A Scale: A B C# D E F# G# A

E Scale: E F# G# A B C# D# E

B Scale: B C# D# E F# G# A# B

Scales with Flats:

F Scale: F G A Bb C D E F

Bb Scale: Bb C D Eb F G A Bb

Eb Scale: Eb G Ab Bb C D Eb

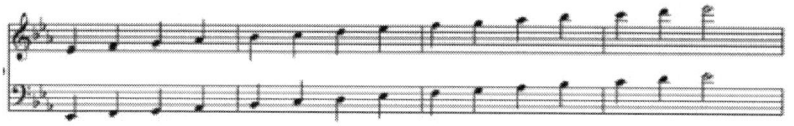

Ab Scale: Ab Bb C Db Eb F G Ab

Db Scale: Db Eb F Gb Ab Bb Cb Db

Test 3: Identify the Scale

1.
2.
3.
4.
5.
6.
7.
8.
9.

Answers on the next page.

Answer to Test 3

1. Ab Scale
2. Bb Scale
3. D Scale
4. A Scale
5. Eb Scale
6. G Scale
7. F Scale
8. C Scale
9. E Scale

Step 5. Read Rhythms and Note Durations

Musical notes have different duration. The time value of notes determines the rhythm of the song.

Italian	English	American	Value	Music Notes
Semibreve	Semibreve	Whole Note	4 Crotchets	𝅝
Minima	Minim	Half Note	2 Crochets	𝅗𝅥
Semiminima	Crotchet	Quarter Note	1 Crotchet	♩
Croma	Quaver	Eighth Note	1/2 a Crotchet	♪
Semicroma	Semiquaver	Sixteenth Note	1/4 a Crotchet	𝅘𝅥𝅯

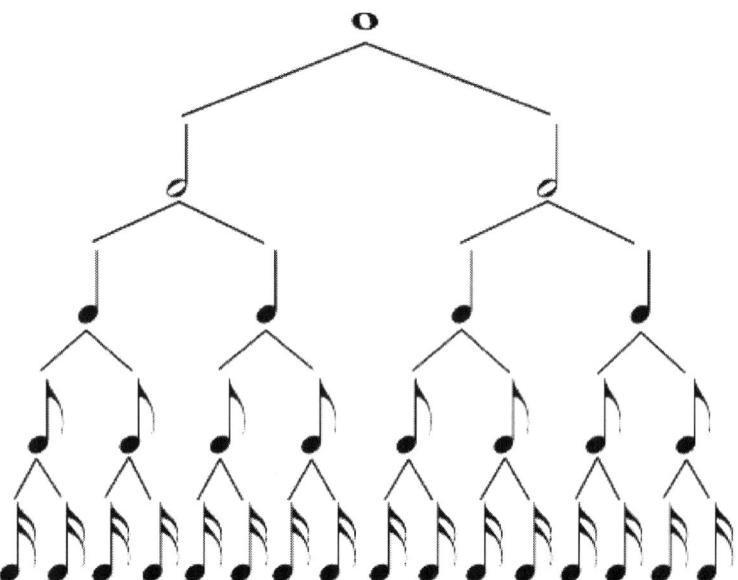

Exercises

Here is a Fun Way for you to Learn Notes Duration:

Whole Note = 4 counts   Dotted Half Note = 3 counts   Half Note = 2 counts   Quarter Note = 1 count

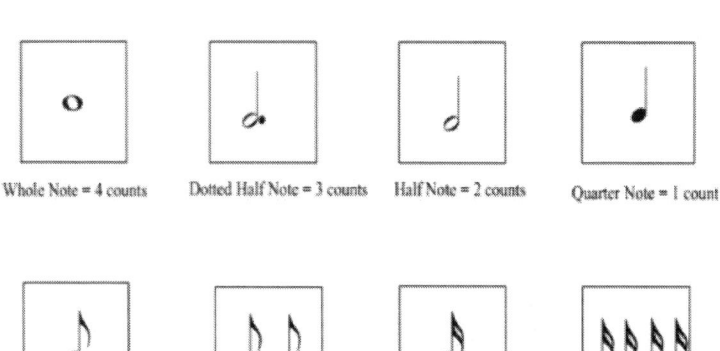

Eighth Note = 1/2 count   2 Eighth Notes = 1 count   Sixteenth Note = 1/4 count   4 Sixteenth Notes = 1 count

Examples:

Use the notes to calculate the mathematical problems:
Isn't this fun?

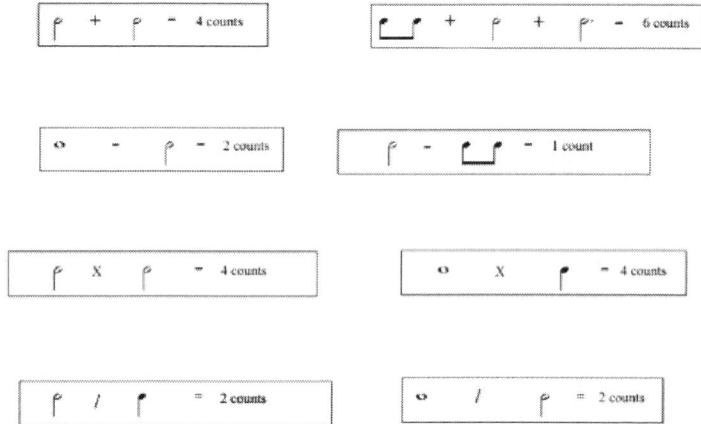

Test 4:

Add up the following notes duration:
Answer is on the next page:

1. 𝅝 + 𝅗𝅥

2. | ♪ ♪ + 𝅗𝅥. − 𝅗𝅥

3. 𝅗𝅥 x 𝅝

4. 𝅗𝅥 x 𝅗𝅥.

5.

6.

7. _____

    ♪♪ ♪♪ + ♩

8.

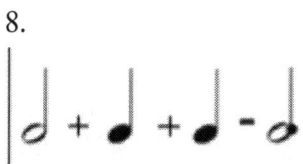

9.

10.

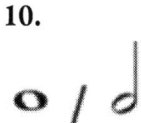

11.

$\d - \eighth\eighth + o$

12.

Answer to Test 4:

1. 6
    2. 2
    3. 8
    4. 6
    5. 13
    6. 1
    7. 2
    8. 1
    9. 4
    10. 2
    11. 5
    12. 14

Step 6. Read Time Signature

The TIME SIGNATURE or metre tells you how the bars are organized. Each piece of music begins with a time signature. It is written as two numbers, one above the other. The upper number tells us the number of beats in a bar. The lower number tells us the value of each beat.

3 beats in a bar
　　Each beat is a quarter note

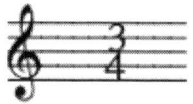

　　3 beats in a bar
　　Each beat is a quarter note

1 2 3	1 2 3	1 2 3	1 2 3
s w w	s w w	s w w	s w w

　　s = strong beat
　　w = weak beat
　　In 3/4 time, the strong beat is on the 1st beat.

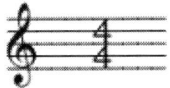

4 beats in a bar
Each beat is a quarter note

1 2 3 4	1 2 3 4	1 2 3 4	1 2 3 4
S W S W	S W S W	S W S W	S W S W

In 4/4 time, the strong beat occurs on the 1st beat and 3rd beat. The 1st downbeat receives a stronger accent than the 3rd beat.

Exercise:

For eg. 4/4 Time Signature - Each bar receives 4 beats:

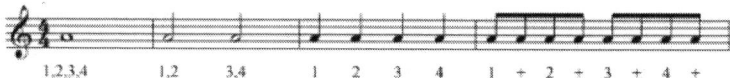

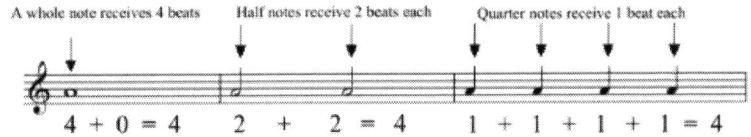

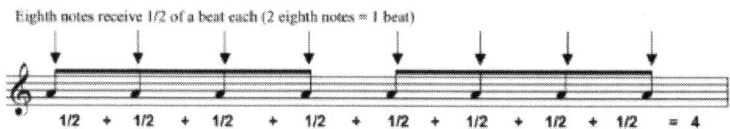

41

Exercises to help you read notes duration within a bar

Example:
Write out the beats underneath the bars: (For a 4/4 time signature, you need 4 beats for each bar)

This is 4/4 song. Can you write out the beats as follows:

You can see that there are 4 beats to a bar - 4/4

Do the following tests yourself:
Write out the 1 2 3 4 underneath the notes.

Test 5:

Answer:

Test 6:

Answer:

Test 7:

Answer:

Step 7. Read the Rests

Rests are periods of silence in a piece of music. When you see a rest, you don't have to do anything. In all rhythm playing, what you do not play is always as important as what you do play, therefore rests are crucial.

The following table shows the relative values of rests.

Italian	English	American	Value	Music Notes
Semibreve Rest	Semibreve Rest	Whole Rest	4 Crotchets	▀
Minima Rest	Minim Rest	Half Rest	2 Crochets	▄
Seminiminima Rest	Crotchet Rest	Quarter Rest	1 Crotchet	𝄽
Croma Rest	Quaver Rest	Eighth Rest	1/2 a Crotchet	𝄾
Semicroma Rest	Semiquaver Rest	Sixteenth Rest	1/4 a Crotchet	𝄿

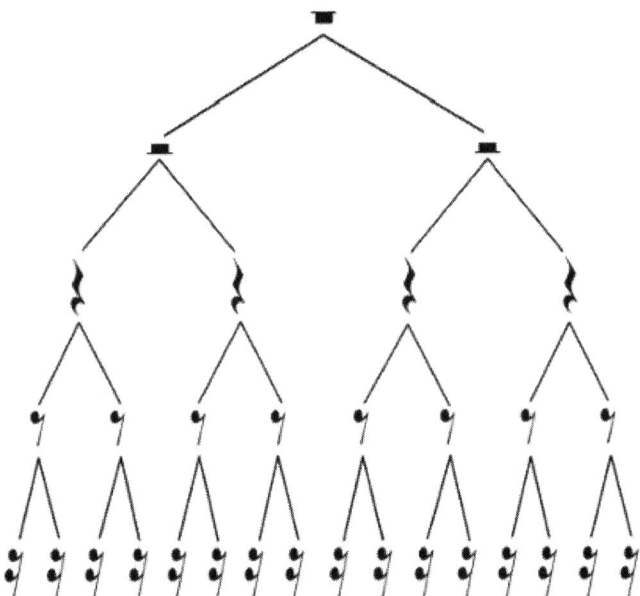

Combining Note Durations & Rests:

When you read music, you need to combine the note durations and rests for them to fit within the bars:

Here is a summary of note durations + Rests:

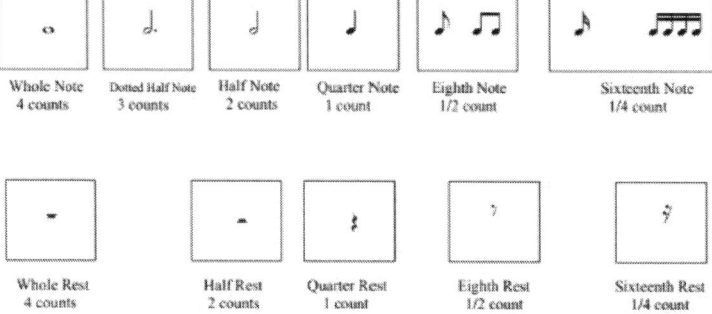

Chapter II Music Note Durations Chart

Note Durations

Double Whole Note

|o|

Whole Note	Whole Rest	Dotted Whole Note	Dotted Whole Rest
o	▬	o.	▬.

Half Note	Half Rest	Dotted Half Note	Dotted Half Rest
♩	▬	♩.	▬.

Quarter Note	Quarter Rest	Dotted Quarter Note	Dotted Quarter Rest
♩	𝄽	♩.	𝄽.

Eighth Note	Eighth Rest	Dotted Eighth Note	Dotted Quarter Rest
♪	𝄾	♪.	𝄾.

Sixteenth Note (16th Note)	16th Rest	Dotted 16th Note	Dotted 16th Rest
♬	𝄿	♬.	𝄿.

32nd Note	32nd Rest	Dotted 32nd Note	Dotted 32nd Rest
♬	𝅀	♬.	𝅀.

Chapter III Music Score Terms Illustrated

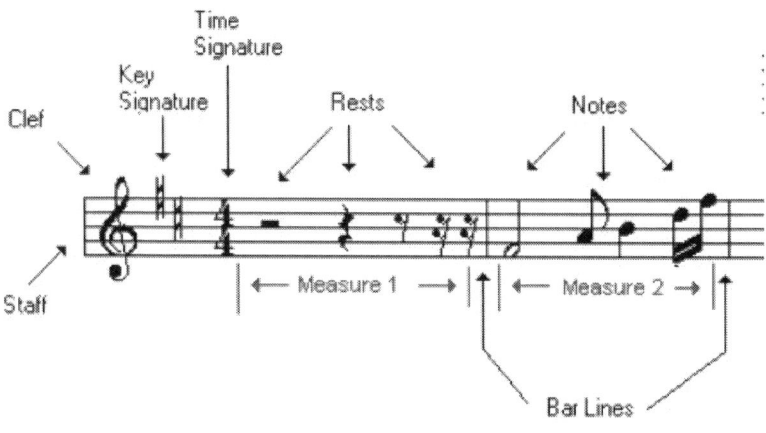

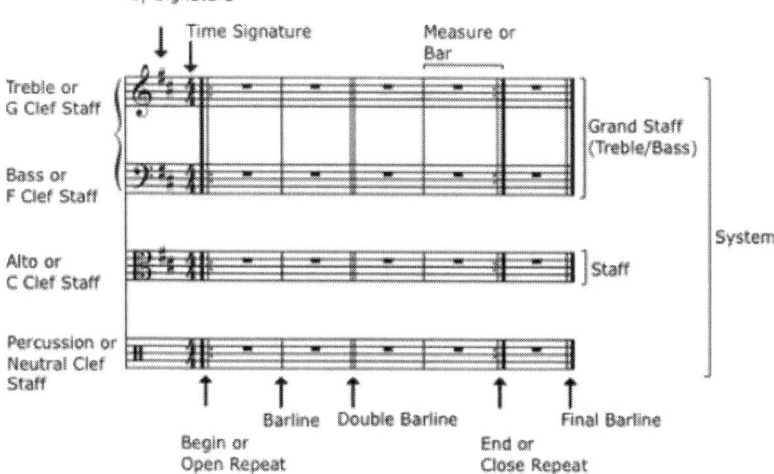

Chapter IV Music Note Terms

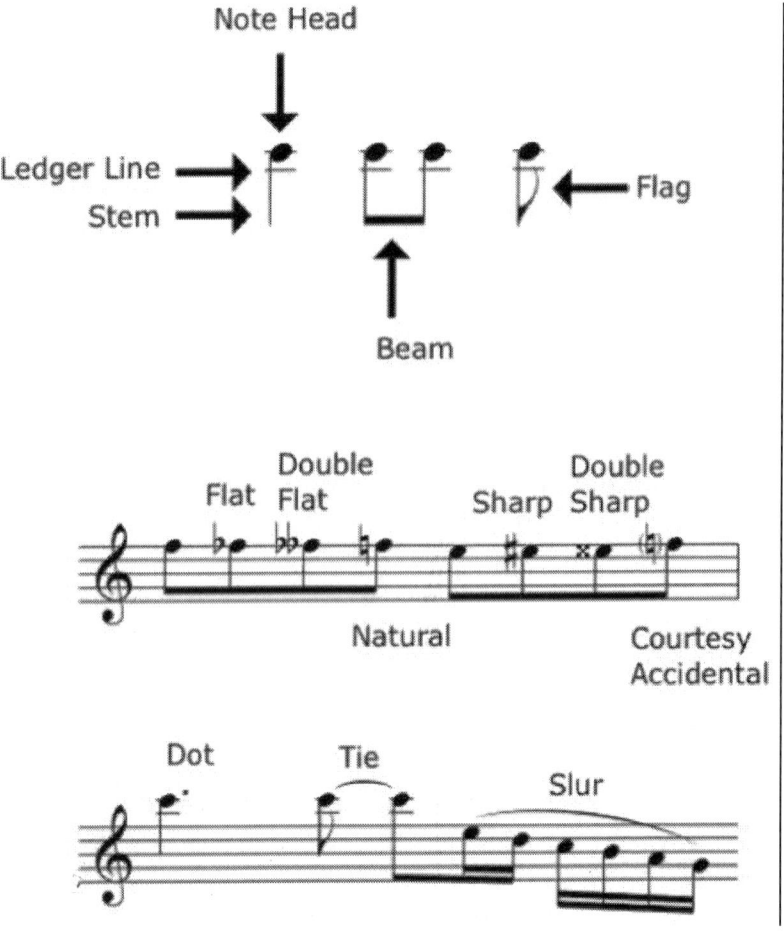

Chapter V Music Dynamics Chart

SIGNS/ SYMBOLS	TERMS	MEANING
p	Piano	Soft
mp	Mezzo Piano	Moderately Soft
pp	Pianissimo	Very Soft
f	Forte	Loud
mf	Mezzo Forte	Moderately Loud
ff	Fortissimo	Very Loud
<	Crescendo (cresc.)	Gradually getting louder.
>	Decrescendo or Diminuendo (dim.)	Gradually getting softer.

Chapter VI 101 Musical Terms

1. **Accompaniment** additional music used to support the melodic line.
2. **A cappella** one or more vocalists performing without an accompaniment.
3. **Arpeggio** a chord with tones that are played successively rather than simultaneously.
4. **Accent** an important aspect of rhythm where the individual notes are emphasized.
5. **Accidental** a note to be played as a flat, sharp, or natural.
6. **Bar** a measure
7. **Bass clef** the lower staff in the grand staff that establishes notes below middle C.
8. **Beat** a regular, recurrent pulsation that divides music into equal units of time.
9. **Bridge** a passage connecting two sections of a composition.
10. **Cadence** the musical punctuation that creates a sense of rest at the end of a phrase.
11. **Cantata** music written for chorus and orchestra. Most often religious in nature.
12. **Capriccio a** quick, improvisational, spirited piece of music.
13. **Chord** a group of three or more tones played simultaneously.

14. **Chord Progression** a sequence of chords moving from one to another in a pattern.
15. **Chromatic** a series of half steps movement.
16. **Clef** a music symbol at the beginning of a staff that determines the pitches.
17. **Consonance** intervals in chords that sound stable; usually points of rest and resolution.
18. **Diatonic** melody built from the seven tones of a major or minor scale.
19. **Dissonance** intervals in chords that sound harsh or unstable.
20. **Dominant** the fifth degree of the diatonic scale.
21. **Downbeat** a strong or accented beat occurring at the first beat of a measure.
22. **Drone** dull, monotonous tone such as a humming or buzzing sound. Also a bass note held under a melody.
23. **Duet** a piece of composition where two people perform together.
24. **Dynamics** refer to the loudness and softness of music.
25. **Embellish** to decorate the melodic line with a variety of sounds and rhythm.
26. **Encore** a piece of music played at the end of a recital responding to the audiences enthusiastic reaction to the performance usually shown by continuous applause.
27. **Enharmonic Interval** two notes that differ in name only. The notes occupy the same position. For example: C sharp and D flat.
28. **Ensemble** the performance of either all instruments of an orchestra or voices in a chorus.
29. **Etude** a musical composition written solely to improve technique, performed for artistic interest.
30. **Exposition** the first section of a movement written in sonata form, introducing the melodies and themes.

31. **Finale** movement or passage that concludes the musical composition.
32. **Flat** a symbol indicating that the note is to be diminished by one semitone.
33. **Form** the overall shape or structure of a piece of music.
34. **Forte** a symbol indicating to play loud.
35. **Fourth** the interval between two notes. Two whole tones and one semitone make up the distance between the two notes.
36. **Frequency** rate of vibration which determines pitch.
37. **Genre** a style of music.
38. **Glissando** a rapid sliding up or down movement from one pitch to another.
39. **Grand staff** a combination of the treble clef and the bass clef.
40. **Groove** the pulse of the song.
41. **Half step** the interval between any two adjacent notes on a keyboard.
42. **Harmony** a pleasing combination of two or three tones played together in the background while a melody is being played. Harmony also refers to the study of chord progressions.
43. **Hymn** a religious song written in several stanzas.
44. **Improvisation** spontaneous musical expression.
45. **Impromptu** a short piano piece, often improvisational and intimate in character.
46. **Intervals** the distance in pitch between any two tones.
47. **Inversion** the rearrangement of the order of chord tones.
48. **Key** refers to a central tone of a piece of music; the keynote or tonality.
49. **Key signature** sharps or flats placed at the beginning of a staff.
50. **Latin rhythm** includes bossa nova, samba, montuno with syncopated rhythmic feel.

51. **Lead sheet** a simple form of music notation with the melody and chords written.

52. **Leading note** the seventh note of the scale where there is a strong desire to resolve on the tonic.

53. **Legato** playing it smooth and connected.

54. **Major** one of the two modes of the tonal system. Music written in major keys have a positive affirming character.

55. **March** a form of music written for marching in two-step time. Originally the march was used for military processions.

56. **Melody** a succession of musical tones varying in pitch and rhythm.

57. **Measure** a rhythmic grouping or metrical unit that contains a fixed number of beats.

58. **Meter** the organization of a strong and weak beat in a recurring pattern.

59. **Midi** an acronym for musical instrument digital interface.

60. **Minor** one of the two modes of the tonal system. The minor mode can be identified by the dark, melancholic mood.

61. **Modulation** when the piece of music moves into a new key.

62. **Motif** the fragment of a theme that forms a melodic, harmonic and rhythmic unit.

63. **Movement** a separate section of a larger composition.

64. **Musicology** the study of forms, history, science, and methods of music.

65. **Natural** a symbol in sheet music that returns a note to its original pitch after it has been augmented or diminished.

66. **Notations** the use of written or printed symbols to represent musical sounds.

67. **Octave** the two tones in which the first pitch is doubled in frequency by the second pitch.

68. **Off-beat** a note that is not on the beat.

69. **Ostinato** a repeated phrase.

70. **Overture** introduction to an opera or other large musical work.

71. **Part** a line in a contrapuntal work performed by an individual voice or instrument.

72. **Partial** a harmonic given off by a note when it is played.

73. **Pentatonic scale** a five-note scale.

74. **Phrase** notes that are connected together in one group.

75. **Pitch** the relative highness or lowness that we hear in a sound.

76. **Pick-up tones** tones that lead to the strong beat of the song.

77. **Prelude** a short piece originally preceded by a more substantial work, also an orchestral introduction to opera, however not lengthy enough to be considered an overture.

78. **Relative pitch** ability to determine the pitch of a note as it relates to the notes that precede and follow it.

79. **Resolution** a movement of sound from dissonance to consonance.

80. **Resonance** when several strings are tuned to harmonically related pitches, all strings vibrate when only one of the strings is struck.

81. **Rest** silence in the piece of music.

82. **Rhythm** the pattern in time created by the duration of individual sounds.

83. **Root** the first tone of a chord.

84. **Score** the complete musical notation of a composition.

85. **Semitone** a half step tone.

86. **Staff** the five horizontal lines on which the music notes are notated.

87. **Subdominant** the fourth degree of the diatonic scale.

88. **Syncopation** when the stress is on the off-beat.

89. **Tempo** the speed of a piece of music; the rate or speed of the beat.

90. **Theme** melodic idea used as a basic building block in the construction of a composition.

91. **Tone** a sound that has a definite pitch.

92. **Tonic** the first degree or central note of the diatonic scale.

93. **Treble clef** the clef in the upper staff that shows pitches above middle C.

94. **Triads** chords of three notes stacked on top of one another in intervals of thirds.

95. **Trill** a quick sequence of two notes played in rapid alteration.

96. **Tritone** a dissonant interval consisting of three whole steps.

97. **Tune** a catchy melody or a song.

98. **Upbeat** a weak or unaccented pulse preceding the downbeat.

99. **Variation** an altered version of a rhythm, motif or theme.

100. **Waltz** a ballroom dance in triple meter.

101. **Whole step** a whole tone.

Printed in Great Britain
by Amazon